A your precious Mother, Ann Davies — a noble woman — whose friendship will ever be a precious treasure

Homemade Joy
from the
House of Jacob

With heartfelt gratitude and love for her light and example of charity. I can't wait to see her again.
Rejoicing Evermore
LaDawn Jacob

# Homemade Joy from the House of Jacob

by
LaDawn Jacob
with Cheryl Carson

Illustrated by
Tamara Howell

Homemade Joy from the House of Jacob

Copyright © 1983 by LaDawn Jacob. All rights reserved. No part of this publication may be reproduced, stored in a retrieval system, or transmitted in any form or by any means, electronic, mechanical, photocopying, recording or otherwise, without prior written permission of the publisher. International rights and foreign translations available only through permission of the publisher.

Cover Illustration by Jon McNaughton. Used by Permission.

Printed in the United States of America

# Dedication

To my eternal companion, Jim, whose faith, love, laughter and multitude of thoughtful acts of service to me and our children have made heaven seem real and reachable.

# Acknowledgments

In writing the thoughts and experiences contained in this book, I have come to more fully realize the extent to which I have been the recipient of the influence and example of my noble parents and heritage. This work is essentially a tribute to my parents, H. Verlan and Shirley Andersen, who gave me life and a desire to live it with joyful gratitude.

They taught me, through their everyday living, that true happiness comes as we strive to conform our lives to the Savior's teachings. They taught me that that which brings the greatest eternal joy takes daily, consistent effort, that in raising children we must believe in the law of the late harvest, as we diligently and tenderly nurture the growing things in our care. Their example has taught me that as I follow the laws that will bring a successful harvest, I may rest assured that my faith and works will surely be rewarded.

To my other parents, Calvin and Ramona Jacob, in whose debt I shall eternally be, for giving life and love and time to prepare a prince of a man to be my eternal companion and father of our children. My deep gratitude to them for their love and support.

I am appreciative of my grandmothers, who deeply influenced my attitudes through their love and teachings. They always made me want to be as special as they seemed to believe I was. The knowledge that I will meet them again one day gives me added incentive to succeed at those things that they taught me were of greatest importance in life.

To my five brothers and five sisters—and to my five sisters and five brothers who married them and made our family

## Acknowledgements

complete—I give special expression of gratitude and love for their patience, faith, and example to me.

To countless loved ones, friends, and associates, whose influence has lifted and sustained and blessed my life. I have known the inexpressible comfort and joy of sharing my heart and of being understood.

I feel gratitude for our nine children and those we hope will yet join our family, for their willingness to come to the House of Jacob and bring an added measure of joy and opportunity for us, their parents, to stretch and grow as we seek to help in the unfolding of each new soul.

Finally, to Cheryl Carson, without whose encouragement, support, and unrelenting efforts this work would have remained indefinitely in the manila folders. Her unselfish friendship has opened up for me a multitude of glorious growing experiences. My love and sincere gratitude to her.

## About the Co-Author

Born sixth in a family of eight children, Cheryl Higginson LeBaron grew up in Nampa, Idaho. She enjoyed a close relationship with her parents, six brothers, and younger sister, having all the advantages of what some would consider poverty.

"But we were rich in that we were taught that we could do or be or accomplish anything if we wanted to badly enough. We children were led to believe that we were loaded with talents, and that all we needed to do in order to excel was to want to."

Cheryl graduated valedictorian of her high school, became first runner-up to Miss Future Business Leader of America for 1969, and received an academic scholarship to Brigham Young University. She attended BYU for two and a half years.

She met Daniel LeBaron at a BYU Devotional, and they were married soon after. She and her husband are the parents of four children: Travis, Stephanie, Allison, and David. They have also cared for eleven foster children in their home for short periods of time. They reside in Orem, Utah.

Cheryl has authored several publications: 'Chastity-Now and Forever'; 'Becoming All That You Are'; 'The Anguish–and Adventure–of Adversity'; and 'Writing an Extraordinary Life Story by an Ordinary Person'. She is a popular lecturer to youth as well as adults, lecturing at BYU Education Weeks, youth conferences, standards events, and firesides.

# How This Book Came to Be

LaDawn was frustrated. She was receiving several letters each day—requests from people asking for copies of her favorite poems, people wanting to know more about the various philosophies and practices of the Jacob household. She was nearing the end of her year as National Young Mother, was starting a new pregnancy, and with nine children, although she wanted to help, it was difficult for her to handle the added stress of all the correspondence, repeatedly having to get copies made of various items, etc.

"If only I could have something already prepared that I could have with me when I speak, or something I could simply slip in the mail!" she wished.

We had already talked of someday writing a book together—just as soon as we got all the children off to college.... But now her need seemed more urgent, especially since her family was preparing to go on tour for a month to eleven different BYU Education Weeks in California. Perhaps something temporary, perhaps a small booklet, would fill the need. Still, we resisted the idea.

Writing, to me, is a painful process. When I had completed my most recent book eight months before, I had heaved a great sigh of relief and said, "It'll be a very long time before I write another book!" I think writing must be like having a baby. In writing, I experience a long period of discomfort, with more exquisite labor pains as the project nears completion and delivery to the printer. I do it only because I am happy to have the results. And since LaDawn, obviously, prefers having babies to writing—nothing was being done.

## How This Book Came to Be

Then, as the anticipated time approached for my husband to return from two months of working out of the state, the realization came to me that I had only one week left. "It's now or never, LaDawn," I said. And so LaDawn took my two-year-old, and I took her manuscript, a piece at a time, and the marathon began.

Initially, it was to be a collection of some of her favorite poems, accompanied by a chapter on family devotionals as well as one dealing with the family's point system. We would reprint the article I had written about LaDawn for a local newspaper in the front of the booklet as an introduction. My sister would do the art work for the cover as well as a few illustrations inside.

But it seemed at first to both of us, to be rather dry and lifeless. I longed for people to be able to know LaDawn as the warm, loving human being that she really is. And so I began listening to the tapes of some of her speeches, transcribing from them excerpts that would illustrate best her personality.

From the time I first became acquainted with LaDawn, I have felt a tremendous amount of respect and admiration for her. It was I who made that fateful phone call that changed her life—as well as the lives of countless women who have been influenced by her great strength and her untiring pursuit of excellence in rearing a successful family. How thrilled I have been to see her reach out and affect so many for good.

As we have become close friends and have shared our innermost feelings, I have found her to be one of the truly valiant, one who loves and desires to please her Father in Heaven. I appreciate her for her openness and her honesty. I know her as a very warm and genuine person, sensitive and caring. She is extremely supportive of others, a real builder of souls.

This is the LaDawn Jacob I had come to know before I ever heard of The Andersen Sisters or the fact that her own children frequently perform. Perhaps because of her enthusiasm in speaking out of her willingness to share talents with others, there have been some who have assumed her to be a "show off." This misjudgment of her motives has caused her some pain.

If there are any parts of this book which may be construed to be boastful in nature, I wish for the reader to know that they were included at my suggestion, not hers. For example, as I was working on the chapter dealing with music, I wondered why LaDawn had not even mentioned her experience as part of The Andersen Sisters sextet. I called: "LaDawn, would you feel uncomfortable if we told about that? I think that people would find it interesting." Only then did she consider and consent to its being included, and she related the story to me by telephone. It was the first time I had ever heard it.

The project continued to grow as new ideas came—additions that seemed unnecessary to make the work complete and the best it could be. It grew from a small booklet to a small book. Hopefully, it will be something of which we can both be proud and glad for. May you feel the zestful spirit of LaDawn Jacob as you enjoy, learn, and are inspired by this, our joint effort, Homemade Joy from the House of Jacob.

Cheryl Carson

## Table of Contents

Dedication

Acknowledgments

About the Co-Author

How This Book Came to Be

### Part I

Chapter I .................................................................... 15

"LaDawn Jacob, National Young Mother of 1982 Reveals Success Secrets"

Chapter II ................................................................... 25

"Nothing That Will Bring You Greater Joy..."

Chapter III .................................................................. 30

A Grateful Heart, A Cheerful Countenance

Chapter IV .................................................................. 36

Becoming America's Young Mother for 1982

### Part II

Chapter V ................................................................... 42

Four Cornerstones for a Sure Foundation

The First Is Love, Then Obedience

Chapter VI .................................................................. 50

Teaching Our Children to Work

Chapter VII ................................................................. 58

Teaching the Gospel of Jesus Christ

*Table of Contents Continued*

## Part III

Chapter VIII ................................................................ 64
  Morningtime, Mealtime, Summertime

Chapter IX .................................................................. 70
  A Love for Learning

Chapter X ................................................................... 74
  The Rich Heritage of Music

## Part IV

Chapter XI .................................................................. 82
  Some of Our Favorite Poems

Post Script: ............................................................... 100

## Chapter I

## "LaDawn Jacob, National Young Mother of 1982 Reveals Success Secrets"
by Cheryl LeBaron
(Reprinted from Central Utah Journal, Feb. 23, 1983)

When the announcement came over the radio last May 1st that LaDawn Jacob of Orem, Utah, had just been named National Young Mother for 1982, her brother was driving across Louisiana. He rolled down his car window and yelled for the world to hear: "She's my sister!"

"She's my sister!" He spoke literally, but numerous women have, figuratively, been able to feel that same sentiment about LaDawn—that sisterhood and that pride—as she has made her unique contribution this year in representing young motherhood in America.

Who is LaDawn Andersen Jacob? If you ask her, she will say: "I'm just an ordinary person; I just feel strongly the importance of the mother. I'm nothing more than anyone else."

She and her husband, James, live in a large home on a residential street. Behind the house stretches the acreage that is part of the farm that LaDawn and her ten brothers and sisters grew up on. Here they keep a cow, chicken, and rabbits. Five of LaDawn's brothers and sisters, now grown, live within a block of their parents' home, though they (H. Verlan and Shirley Andersen) are currently away, serving an LDS mission in Argentina.

What has this past year been like for this mother of nine—all boys except for seven of them—ranging in age from 12 years to 15 months? How has she and her family coped with the added opportunities and responsibilities that have come with her title?

When my husband and I visited LaDawn's home one evening last week, it was the end of a long day for her. She greeted us warmly as always, however, her sparkling eyes and a bright smile lighting her face. Then she said in dismay, "I'm not at all a person to write an article about, especially tonight. How can I tell anyone about anything? After a day like today, you might say in your article, 'LaDawn Jacob is open to any and all suggestions...'"

It seems the day had gotten off to a bad start. They had slept late and had gotten up at 5:30 a.m. instead of the normal 5:00 a.m. She had gone jogging, later, while her husband was taking a shower. ("What were the children doing?" I asked.) "They were racing through the house, throwing Loc Blocs." And to top it all off, she had later spanked her little boy twice with the wooden spoon—the very wooden spoon that he (and his dad) had made for her in Cub Scouts. ("How can you use that on me when I'm the one who made it for you?")

LaDawn showed us through their home—1800 square feet on each of three levels, though the basement is not finished. Because of the size of the rooms, some of them appear rather sparsely furnished. "This house if very functional, not fancy," she explained.

From the living room she led us into what was originally designed to be the formal dining room but which serves as the Music Room. A baby grand piano (the one LaDawn grew up with) sits in the center. Shelves along one wall hold violins and other instruments. "And this is my favorite piece of furniture," LaDawn says, as she opens a cupboard built with 18 different compartments which hold the different music books for the different children and their different instruments. "It has helped so much to have things organized."

Into the large kitchen—with the several quarts of apples she had bottled that day, the empty gallon bottles on the counter waiting to be filled with milk the next morning, the eggs lying on the towel to dry.

Beyond the kitchen is the dining area and then the family room with its wood-burning stove and stovetop-sized pancake griddle. A small table and chair set in the middle of the room is the site for the nursery school she conducts for the four- and two-year olds. Covering one wall area is the large mirror which the children use to practice their actions as they work on their routines for performing, which the family does together. (There are handprints on only the bottom half of the mirror.)

Upstairs are the five large bedrooms. As we enter each room, LaDawn turns off the BYU game coming over the intercoms, for the children are all fast asleep, (though I suspect the one wiggling her foot is only pretending to be asleep.) Because their day begins so early, the children's bedtime is 8:00 p.m. After they are in bed, LaDawn sits in the hallway between the bedrooms and reads to her children. Last year they read Shakespeare. ("Children are like sponges; they can absorb anything you feed into them.")

What makes a typical day in the House of Jacob? I must preface the account by saying that the Jacobs have expressed a concern that others might get the impression they feel the Jacob way is the only right way. "As I contemplate how this will appear to others, I am overwhelmed by how crazy it all sounds. Nobody will even believe that we have six children practicing their music all at the same time.... And for most families, to get up at the time we do would be totally insane!" Enough said.

## Homemade Joy from the House of Jacob

Jim and LaDawn arise very early. Jim usually awakens the oldest four children (12, 11, 10 and 9), helping them make their beds as they roll out of them. He and the older son then go out and milk the cow (the girls take turns for the evening milking), while the three girls and LaDawn get dressed. Mother starts to pack the eight lunches and cooks breakfast. They always have some kind of mush, or cooked cereal.

Next, LaDawn practices music with the three oldest girls, who sing together in a trio. The girls then each do their own practicing, two on violin, one on cello. Jim then comes in and LaDawn finishes making the breakfast and lunches while still overseeing practicing, since the Music Room is just off the kitchen.

Music is very important in the Jacob household. The children practice their various instruments in the mornings and do their piano practicing after school. (The Jacobs have two pianos.) They take lessons from others for their various instruments, but LaDawn teaches them piano herself. Their oldest daughter, the seventh grader, also teaches violin lessons and helps teach music at her school.

Jim wakes up the younger children by 6:00... at least those who are still sleeping through the practicing. LaDawn generally dresses the "babies" while Jim strains the milk. Their son is sitting at the counter in the kitchen, practicing his guitar, while Dad sings along: "'Let me be there in your morning'..." The six- and seven- year-old girls unload the dishwasher and set the table. Then they begin their own practicing—on the harp and the violin—in different ends of the living room. (The cello and violin are still playing in the background.)

Breakfast begins at 7:15 or 7:30 a.m. Then the family all gathers in the living room for a 15-20 minute devotional. They sing a hymn, work on learning a scripture, then spend a few minutes memorizing a poem. Even the six-year-old can

## "LaDawn Jacob, National Young Mother of 1982"

flawlessly recite the 32 lines of "My Kingdom" by Louisa May Alcott.

The school-age children all "run out the door" at 8:00 a.m. Jim, an accountant, leaves for work just before 9:00 a.m. LaDawn cleans up the kitchen and then goes with the flip charts to inspect the work assignments of the children, the specific areas of the house for which each child has a responsibility. (They rotate work assignments every nine months.)

The Jacob family works with a system in which points are earned for various tasks (10 points for unloading the dishwasher, 15 for folding a load of laundry), or subtracted for misdeeds such as leaving belongings out. Extra point bonuses and incentives such as going out to eat for a week of perfect practicing are also used. The points are converted to money (each point equals a penny), and from this the child pays for his own music lessons, clothing, and other necessities as well as fun things (after the 10% tithing and 20% for savings are taken out). "Parents have to come up with the money for the needs of their children one way or another," says LaDawn. "We have found this worked very well. We have also found we have to keep changing all the time; children get tired of always having the same incentives."

Jim continued to explain. "Our home life may seem to be extremely organized, and a lot of people may not feel comfortable being so regimented. But with this many people, we feel we need it this way." He smiled. "We look at it this way: one could go crazy from being too organized, or one could go crazy from a lack of organization. We prefer it this way."

LaDawn feeds the children supper as soon as they get home from school, an idea picked up from a book by Mormon Church leader Boyd K. Packer. That way, they can get on with their afternoon and evening projects, happy and well fed, rather than hungry or asking for snacks. Jim doesn't mind eating his dinner alone when he comes home later. "The children are usually all buzzing around, so I'm not really alone," he laughed.

LaDawn added: "Dads are really important in the functioning of a good home. A father who is supportive and involved in the rearing of the children makes it happier and so much more successful. It is so much harder to do it alone, without that support. And it helps when you both have similar goals."

The family has what they refer to as "The Ten Commandments of the House of Jacob," a list of ten rules and appropriate consequences for breaking them. (For example, carrying food onto the carpeting gets the consequence of getting to vacuum, whether or not any food is spilled.) Commandment Number One is: "Thou shalt be cheerful." Then LaDawn quoted a little ditty:

> *Be pretty if you are;*
> *Be witty if you can;*
> *But be cheerful if it kills you.*

I asked LaDawn what would happen if the many, many poems she has memorized over the years were suddenly erased from her mind. She thought a brief moment and laughed: "I'd probably be speechless!"

None can mistake LaDawn's vitality, her enthusiasm for mothering. Her eyes light up every time she talks of it. What are her feelings about being selected as National Young Mother Representative?

"I feel as though I was plucked out of obscurity—but at the same time, I can see how I was being prepared for a long time....The interest I had, the strong feelings about the importance of mothering...for years I have studied the influence of the mother in the home, the significance of the

## "LaDawn Jacob, National Young Mother of 1982"

early childhood years, the mother as the child's first and most important teacher.

"I had very strong feelings about things because of my background. My mother and grandmothers had all instilled in me the knowledge that the most important contribution I could make in life was to raise a successful family, and that nothing would bring greater joy or satisfaction in this life and all the eternities. I was raised in a home where children were valued and cherished, where they were truly considered assets, not liabilities. I believe that that attitude enables a mother and father to be strong through the trying times, the challenging times."

What have been some of the highlights of her year as National Young Mother? Jim said, "The state and then the national conventions (where she received the awards) were very exciting."

"There was the trip back to Lincoln, Nebraska, with our family where we sang and performed in several cities as well as in Cheyenne and Denver." LaDawn returned to Denver for the national board meeting of American Mothers and was thrilled to be able to spend time with Barbara B. Smith, President of the LDS Relief Society, who is on the national board; they traveled home to Salt Lake City together.

In three weeks she will go to Butte, Montana. And in May the entire family will be flown again to Denver. (Most trips have been at their own expense, however.) And then the National American Mothers' Convention will be held in New York City in April, where LaDawn will relinquish her title.

How does her family handle her being away? "When I come home, everything is in order, the laundry is all done.... I feel as though I'm not so indispensable after all." She laughed. "I may as well leave, Jim handles things so well when I'm gone. But that's the kind of guy he is."

## Homemade Joy from the House of Jacob

Jim looked at her and said quickly, "We were really glad to see you come home."

LaDawn continued. "As for the experiences I've had, most satisfying to me has been the appreciation that mothers seem to feel when I share my ideas with them. They say, 'I can't believe what a difference this has made in our family. We are so much happier—our children are doing this and this....' That makes me feel so good to know that they can use these ideas in their own homes. But all I am doing is sharing ideas that I have learned from others."

Added LaDawn, "I wish I were creative like my sister-in-law. When her husband had settled in to watch television while she was feeling hassled trying to get the children to bed, she thought to take a lovely silver platter and drape bunches of grapes over it. Presenting it to him, she said sweetly, 'Is there anything else I can do to make you more comfortable, Dear?' He got the message, jumped up, and helped her with the children."

She continued, "I have been the beneficiary of so many outstanding people who have been a great influence on my life. I am a sponge. I guess that is why I am so fanatical about memorizing—I get strength from others. The idea for learning a hymn in our devotionals came from my sister, scripture memorizing from my parents. I learned that Paul H. Dunn's Sunday School teacher used to have them memorize good poetry, so I thought, 'Why not do that with my own children?' I thrive on other people's knowledge and like to apply ideas from them in my own home and in my own life...and then to share my knowledge with others."

As for her philosophy toward womanhood and mothering: "In visiting with other women, I see a tremendous amount of talents and abilities and intelligence, compassion and love. They have so much that they can offer and give to their

## "LaDawn Jacob, National Young Mother of 1982"

families: their own unique selves. I think it is very important for women to really feel a sense of appreciation for their own special individuality.

"It is a challenge to teach children responsibility, to teach them to work, to be obedient. It takes a tremendous amount of time to teach children the character traits they'll need to succeed in life. Children have to be taught and shown, not just told. That's where the real parental teaching and training comes.... There are no quicky devices for raising children, as there are today in other areas of life. In times past, children worked right alongside their parents and learned by their very lifestyle. Nowadays they have to be consciously taught."

"It's been fun taking our children around and letting them perform, having such good visual aids as I speak to people about teaching and raising children. Having your children say the poems they've learned, or play, or sing, is an example right there, in living color. Our children have a lot of confidence and poise. Those things don't happen by accident."

LaDawn Jacob. Happy person. Intelligent and talented. Successful wife, mother of nine. Representing the ideals of mothers everywhere as National Young Mother for 1982. I, too, can feel the pride of her own brother expressed: "She's my sister!"

*Homemade Joy from the House of Jacob*

## Chapter II

## "Nothing That Will Bring You Greater Joy..."

From my birth as the fourth of twelve children, I felt loved and cherished. Added to that, a significant event occurred when I was twelve that further enlarged and deepened those feelings.

When my youngest brother was brought home from the hospital—number twelve—it was on Thanksgiving Day. I remember standing at the windows, all of us, our noses pressed against the windowpanes, waiting for our old station wagon to come down to Washboard Lane carrying Mama and Daddy and the new baby.

I remember as it finally came, how my heart pounded with joy and how thrilled I felt. They drove in the driveway and Daddy and Mama came in the door.... I still recall Mama's long, pink robe. (It was in the days when women stayed in the hospital for more than five minutes.)

And as they came in the door, I remember my father calling us together and having us kneel down around our front room table. And there my father expressed a special prayer of gratitude to the Lord for this tiny infant that had come to join our family.

I experienced the overwhelming feeling then that the best thing the Lord could do was to send a baby to a home.

And so you see, don't blame Jim and me for all the children! It was bred into me that children were a blessing, that children were an asset, not a liability. I never remember thinking that children were even an expense, but only a glorious blessing. And for that, I am so very grateful.

I have often reflected upon the idea that if new, young parents realized when they received their first child what a huge responsibility they were taking on, there would probably be fewer parents in the world. (And perhaps if the baby realized how inexperienced and naive his parents were, he would probably refuse to go home with them from the hospital!)

On the other hand, if these parents could even partially comprehend the joy and satisfaction that comes from rearing children successfully, we would, perhaps, be willing to put forth even greater effort and time to achieve the goal.

The greatest help and blessing to me as a mother has been, without a doubt, the example of my own mother. Her untiring sacrifice, giving of her time and energy in behalf of her children, continues to be an inspiration to me.

She always made us feel that having children was the greatest thing we could do, and we are all stretching ourselves, trying to follow in her footsteps.

I also had a wonderful grandma who used to say to me, "LaDawn, there is nothing that will bring you greater joy in this life and all the eternities than your family."

There was a time when we had five little children, all preschoolers. In fact, we had three in diapers at the same time. I used to run through the house and say, "Bottoms up, everyone; bottoms up!" I couldn't remember which diaper I had changed, but I knew someone needed their diaper changed every minute!

I had quite a struggle at times, and I remember hollering at my children and of thinking, "Where did you all come from?" and "What's a nice girl like me doing in a place like this?" I remember wondering if all of my life would be spent changing and washing diapers and wiping noses, and finding shoes and socks that matched.

One of my greatest concerns was that I knew my grandma could see me from heaven, as she had passed away a short time before. I worried a great deal about what she must think of me, being mean and ornery and hollering at my children and all. She must be thinking, "How horrible!" I wasn't anything like she had thought I was.

One night I went to bed, and during the night, I had a dream. In this dream I was in a very large home, back in a bedroom. Someone came to my door and said, "LaDawn, your grandma is here to see you."

## Homemade Joy from the House of Jacob

I rushed to the top of the stairs and looked down, and there was my grandma, as radiant and beautiful as she had been in life. I ran down the stairs and she enfolded me in her arms and held me to her, and I felt the warmth of her body. Then she took me by the shoulders and stood me back one step and looked into my eyes and smiled into my face. It was as if she were saying to me: "LaDawn, I understand. I know what you're feeling and I love you and I'm proud of you. And you keep trying, and things will come out all right."

From that beautiful experience, I knew that Grandma understood. I knew she loved me, and I knew that she had compassion, that she didn't think I was awful at all. She loved me.

And I have often thought, "Wouldn't it be wonderful to live for the day that we can return again to the presence of our Heavenly Father and Heavenly Mother and have them put their arms around us and hold us close to them and look into their eyes and smile.

Oh, if we could but live for that day! You must know that the Lord loves you and understands every trial and tribulation that you experience. He knows and He understands, and He loves you. Have faith, believing that He wants more than anything else for you to return to him.

## Chapter III

## A Grateful Heart, A Cheerful Countenance

One of the qualities I have grown to appreciate most about my heritage is their possessing the attitude of gratitude. My grandmothers were both living examples of this quality in their own lives, never seeming to feel or see anything except all of the blessings they were abundantly given. My parents, raised in homes where "being thankful" was part of living, were imbued with this delightful trait that makes life so happy.

My Grandmother Andersen, who had such a tremendous influence on my life, used to say, "I spend half of my time counting my blessings and the other half thanking the Lord for them, and that leaves no time to feel sorry for myself."

Near the end of her life as her body was wasted away with cancer and she lay on her bed, weak and in a considerable amount of pain, my own mother leaned over and expressed the wish that somehow they could relieve Grandma of some of the burden and the pain she was experiencing. Grandma looked up and smiled in a most reassuring way and said, "Shirley, this is such a small thing to go through for one who has been blessed as much as I. The Lord has been so good to me."

I said to myself, "Blessed!?" I thought of her life as a widow for nearly 40 years, the mother of ten children, raising many of them alone after the death of her husband. She had endured the loss of two homes, one in a flood, and one when they were driven from Mexico. She had lived much of her life in what might be considered dire poverty. Yet, to her, the Lord had blessed her beyond measure, for all she could see were the blessings. Such was her grateful heart.

Oh, that each of us could have a heart full of gratitude! I have yet to meet a grateful person who was not happy. Those who have the ability to see their blessings feel joy in life, even through difficult times. In my association with many fine people, those who seem to find unlimited satisfaction in the process of living are those whose hearts are most often filled with appreciation for life. Life is so much richer and fuller, as we are able to savor every experience with gusto.

A grateful heart doesn't complain at not having the whole orchestra, but rejoices in the celestial strains of one violin.

We have each been in a situation where a gift we had lovingly given was appreciated; we glowed with happiness and felt a desire to give again. I'm sure we have also known the disappointment of giving and realizing that our work was hardly noticed.

In preparing meals for my family, I have ample opportunity to test this out. If my children complain about my efforts to produce a nutritious and tasty meal, I determine to serve them nothing but bread and gravy the next night.

I have often wondered if perhaps the Lord may not also get tired of providing feasts for us and having us complain because there was no salt on the peas. Perhaps the reason we are unable to receive more fully the blessings of the Lord is that we are not appreciative of what we have.

We are so blessed to be alive, blessed to be women. I hope you feel that way, that you are glad to be who you are. One of the most important things that women need to possess, I feel, is the attitude of a grateful heart. Oh, be grateful!

I once asked Barbara B. Smith, General President of the Relief Society, what women in the church needed most. She replied, "First, to be founded in the scriptures; and second, they need to have more grateful hearts."

Too many of us don't appreciate our blessings. We complain about this and we complain about that. I wish I could do this, or I'm unhappy that I can't do that. My husband has smelly socks, and my kids don't mind. We seem to have so much to complain about.

Perhaps we should spend more time in our family and personal prayers letting our Heavenly Father know that we do feel appreciation for His multitude of blessings to us. Some prayers may be almost wholly prayers of thankfulness, prayers of praise and rejoicing.

Our children should hear us express daily—many times daily—our gratitude for the many little joys and blessings of life. Attitude is caught, not taught, and the attitude of gratitude is no exception.

If you don't feel the depth of appreciation you would like, pray to have that feeling magnified. Think often of your blessings, "name them one by one," share them with others, sing of them, talk of them and truly appreciate them, and you will find your life noticeably enriched and blessed.

Oh, the inexpressible joy of associating with those who have taken literally the admonition to "be of good cheer." What a blessing is the home where members go forward to light up those around them rather than to put out lights.

Contrary to what some may suppose, however, those with a ready smile did not come ready-made. Though attitude makes a big difference in one's ability to see something to smile about, it is the individual who must ultimately desire to acquire that wonderful trait.

My mother and father were both happy people. I never remember my mother waking us up with a sour face although, considering her nearly nine years of nausea associated with the bearing of 12 children, I am amazed at her stamina. She would come in, even after nights of being up with sick babies, her eyes bleary, but with a smile and a song. As I moaned over the prospects of "getting up and at it," I failed at the time to appreciate that noble act she performed each morning of being cheerful despite how she really must have felt inside.

One of our most important rules in our own home is to "Be Cheerful," with some corresponding advice: "If you're happy, notify your face." Also, "if you can't turn the corners of your mouth up, let the middle sag." I often tell the children that the most important thing you wear out of the house is a smile—and that goes for inside the house, too.

A great incentive for developing a cheerful disposition is that our face takes on, as the years go by, the appearance of what is within our hearts. If we are sour and grumpy, our faces soon match up to our insides. If, on the other hand, we are cheerful and joyous within, we become more beautiful and radiant in our faces. Something to think about!

In a society that takes great pains and efforts to stress the need to "look" good and be "in," we must teach with great emphasis in our homes that, as the Lord told Samuel (speaking of David), "Look not on his countenance or on the height of his stature...for the Lord seeth not as man seeth; for man looketh on the outward appearance, but the Lord looketh upon the heart."

It is good to remind ourselves that the Lord will not judge us on where we buy our clothes, or what brand we wear, but rather what is in our hearts. As parents we need to value our children for those qualities of love and service and goodness that will endure long after the heels and hose and Calvin Klein jeans have lost their appeal. Teach them the importance of developing a character that rings with joy and gratitude and cheerfulness even when those around them preach that happiness is in having the "latest" or the "neatest".

In our own lives, our cheerfulness is contagious. Research indicates that those who laugh easily have no need to worry about high blood pressure. Learn to laugh and see the humor in the little experiences that happen. Learn to "have a laugh" when the milk spills, when the children and chaos get past the point of endurance. Your light will be the flame to light other lights, and the whole world will be brighter for your having been here.

# Chapter IV

## Becoming America's Young Mother For 1982

It has been a thrilling and exciting and a glorious year. I have loved championing the cause of Young Mothers.

But when I was initially contacted one day by telephone and asked if I would consider being nominated as Young Mother for Utah from our area, I laughed. I said, "I'm very sorry, but my four-year-old still wets her pants.... Right now the children are throwing peas at each other across the table...etc."

"But LaDawn," the caller persisted, "you really believe in mothering.... And you know how important you are." I agreed. (With nine children, you'd better believe in it!) "On that basis, then, would you allow your name to be placed in nomination?"

I was, over the next few weeks, involved in preparing the necessary materials: essays on my philosophy of parenting, a biographical sketch, letters of recommendation, etc., to be considered by the judges.

I was contacted several weeks later: "LaDawn, you have been chosen to represent Utah." To be honest, I didn't know whether to laugh or to cry. But I decided I'd cry. I told my husband it just wasn't fair because—well, he knew the way the kids acted in church as well as I did! He knew the children have, on occasion, run out the door and down the street, bare naked! How could they do this to me? I imagined that every time one of my children misbehaved, people would say, "And she's the Young Mother of the Year?!"

I was moaning and groaning to my mother one night, saying, "I just don't see how it is possible, how it can be done.

I'm not capable of doing that. I don't belong on that kind of a pedestal."

I went to the mailbox three days later, and there was a letter from my mother. (My parents were at the Mission Training Center in Provo, learning Spanish in preparation for their departure for a mission to Argentina.) I have been carrying this letter with me all year:

*Dear LaDawn,*

*I have been thinking and praying, and I don't have any profound wisdom to give you. But perhaps having experienced some of the same things, at least I can truly say that I understand. And if I could lift the load and bear some of it for you, I would.*

*I know the Lord will bless you and that nothing is impossible with the Lord. Some way, somehow, you will be given strength, and others will come to your aid.*

*LaDawn, you have earned so many blessings. And I know your Heavenly Father loves you. He will give you the strength and the wisdom to do what you are called to do.*

And I have found in my life this past year the fulfillment of this. The Lord truly has come to my aid and given me abilities and capacities that I have not had before.

And the very best thing He has given me is a wonderful companion and dear husband who made a commitment that when I was gone speaking, that he would be home with the children. He has been a sheep rancher before, and he has often made the statement, "It's easier to bed down 5,000 ewes than nine children..." I have been so blessed by wonderful support. My grandma always called him a prince of a man, that is just what he is.

And so, as Utah's Young Mother Representative, I attended the National Convention for American Mothers, Inc., held in Salt Lake City. It was a marvelous experience; I felt like Cinderella going to the ball. We stayed on the top floor of the Hotel Utah, and each morning as I awakened and saw out the window the Angel Moroni blowing his trumpet atop the nearby LDS Temple, I'd wonder if I'd died and gone to heaven!

I had taken two of my older daughters with me to tend the baby while I was attending the sessions. I was nursing the baby, so I needed her to be with me; we were inseparable companions at that time.

The day before the announcement was to be made, some of the state Young Mother Representatives were visiting and said, "LaDawn, did you know what they were judging you on?"

I replied, "No, but I know it wasn't my figure."

They said, "Did you know that there have been judges circulating during the convention, observing?" I thought of how during a meeting I would go to the back of the room, throw a blanket over me, and nurse my baby. I'll bet they were really impressed!

One woman mentioned how they never select, as national winner, a mother who has several young children at home. (I thought, "Strike one.") And they did not want a Mormon, because there had been a disproportionately large number of Mormon women selected in the past. ("Strike two," I thought.)

And they did not want someone from Utah, since the convention was being held there. ("Strike three; I'm out.") That night I went to bed feeling very sorry that Utah Young Mothers had chosen a real loser to represent them.

The next day was the Announcement Ceremony at a special luncheon in the Hotel Utah. It was just beautiful. I had gotten a ticket for my husband, and after the ceremony, we planned to return to Orem to resume raising our children, growing tomatoes, milking the cow, and the other everyday things we were involved in.

My husband was a little late. "How are the children?"

"Oh, they're fine. In fact, I brought them with me."

"You did what?"

As the dinner progressed and they had made the announcement of the Mother of the Year, then a cameraman moved over and positioned himself directly in front of our table. "Aha! It's someone at our table!" (I was aware of how they sometimes tip off the cameraman in advance so he can capture the reaction of the winner as she is announced.) I selected, mentally, a couple of women there who I thought it might be...

And then they announced the National Young Mother Representative for 1982: LaDawn Jacob of Utah. My first thought was that they had made a terrible mistake. And so I held back for a moment, not wanting to go up and accept anything. I honestly thought they were going to say, "Oh, my goodness; we've made a mistake! We have said the wrong name; it is someone else."

But the cameras were flashing, I was being presented with roses, the children were coming in. UPI interviewed me afterward. There was no mistake.

And there were the children!

Not to slight my wonderful husband, but there are three things that he has difficulty with. One of these is: it is hard for him to tell when things are color-coordinated. (Red socks and a purple dress are fine.) Another: he is not adept at combing girls' hair. And the third: he has a hard time telling which things fasten in the back and which the front.

And so, as dearly as I love my children, my biggest concern as they came in that day while all the cameras were flashing, was that perhaps one would have on mismatched socks and one's hair wouldn't be combed, and one's hem might be out of a dress, or it might be backwards.... And my fears were... valid.

But the wonderful part of all that was the fact that as they came into the room, I kept hearing people gasping and saying, "Nine children!" (Gasp) "Nine children!" (Gasp) "Nine children!"

And I thought, "They are so overcome with the quantity, that they will not even notice the quality." So on all counts, we are saved!

Then it was announced that the Jacob children frequently perform, and would they come up and perform for everyone? They did, and were given a standing ovation. Then someone whispered, "Why don't you have them sing, 'I Am a Child of God'?" So they sang 'I Am a Child of God' and 'Families Can Be Together Forever,' and there were many tears shed by the women there in the audience.

I had the feeling then that I knew Heavenly Father had a purpose for my doing what I was doing—not for myself, but for His work and His glory—for the opportunity of sharing the message of the eternal family with other people.

It has been a tremendous experience for me.

# Chapter V

## Four Cornerstones for a Sure Foundation
## The First is Love, Then Obedience

Shortly after the birth of our first daughter, I remember feeling an overwhelming realization come to me. "I will be a mother forever and ever." It seemed impossible that in one small, earthly moment, the bestowal of that title could be given, and I suddenly felt an awe. It was though a gentle, yet heavy, mantle enveloped me, and I knew that life, through all the eternities, would never be the same.

As I mentioned earlier, as a child I often heard my Grandma Andersen tell me, "LaDawn, there is nothing that will bring you greater joy in this life and all the eternities than your family." That seemed reasonable enough and yet, it seemed like such a long journey from where I was, there in the hospital, to the completion of that promise. How would I know what to do, which road to take, what to teach, so that the eternal joy that was promised through families would be mine?

There have been times, in the midst of the confusion at the table, children tussling on the floor, a child in the high chair daintily dropping food onto the floor, and one whining at my side, that I have wondered about the "joy" of the experience.

On hearing the little adage, "Home is a bit of heaven here on earth," I have seriously thought that if heaven was to be like this, maybe I really didn't want to go there, after all. Then, too, I have many times felt in our home rejoicing at the love and laughter there.

Now, through a heavenly miracle, we are parents. And blessed with other heavenly miracles, we may be successful parents.

I have found much help from the example of my own precious parents, who provided us living proof that righteousness is the pre-requisite to happiness. I observed and learned from other successful families and have listened and read and searched and prayed for help.

The journey, to Jim and me, though still long and difficult, seems to have giant road signs to direct our efforts. We now have definite ideas about those values we must teach, the character traits that must be developed, and the principles we must live by.

Then, too, we have the knowledge that our Father in Heaven knows our child far better than we do. He is so deeply

desirous that His child return to Him that He is very close, reaching out to lend His love and help that we, together, might bring this child back to His presence. What a great comfort this knowledge brings!

As mothers, our work is not washing dishes and mending holes. Our work is rearing children. But it is much more than that. For we rear our children to be successful, to fulfill their potential. The little people with whom we share our homes are more than gifts from God; they are gods in embryo, themselves. Our work is to help them realize that awe-inspiring fact and then to live so that they will not fall short of their divine potential."

I feel that there are four basic cornerstones that are essential in the building of each child's immortal home, his soul. Many other virtues add beauty to his home, but in order to make the building stand the winds and storms of mortality, he must have a solid foundation based on these things:

1—Love
2—Obedience
3—Work
4—The Gospel of Jesus Christ


There. After seeing them all together, that formula doesn't look nearly so formidable as might have thought. True, there are large stones to lay, and there are various ways they each may be taught, but now we know, at least, what direction to take.

## LOVE

Love is, of course, the foundation for all happy homes. It is important that children feel loved, even before birth. Love them before they come, and love them after they come.

I am always shocked when I hear parents say, "We don't want any more children," or, "This is our last, I hope," or "This one is our 'accident!'" That is, not only a blow to the child of whom they are speaking, but to each child in that home, as well. On the other hand, when children hear their parents express to others their delight and pride in having this special child a part of their family, what a different attitude that child will have about his own unique importance.

My parents always expressed love for us during family prayer and often named the needs of the individual children, asking for a special blessing in their behalf. And when they mentioned to the Lord their gratitude for their children's desires to be obedient, it made me want to be just that. Let your children hear you express love for them often.

A child is never too old to need and bask in the warmth of a parent's hugs and kisses and pats on the back. "Keep in touch." Research indicates that children who are hugged more seem to be healthier as they grow up; this is even more dramatically evidenced in adulthood. (A good way to cut down on medical expenses, perhaps.)

When my daddy would ask me, as a little girl, if I had a kiss for him that day, I used to try to count up in my mind how many I had given out, for I thought I was only allotted a certain number and did not want to run out too early. How happy I was to learn that I could give kisses and hugs to Daddy and Mommy and all my brothers and sisters without reservation, or at least a long as they would let me! Don't act as though you'll run out. You'll find your capacity to give only increases as you are willing to share what you have.

There have been times when the demands on my ability to give love have seemed to drain my reserves. It is important as a parent to pray daily for an increased ability to love. We must "weary the Lord" with our petitioning for this gift. As we live closer to Him, and as we truly desire this increase of love in our hearts, we will be blessed with that "greatest of all the gifts of God." Love truly does "conquer all"—so use it!

I began to realize some months ago that there were days when my oldest children got only one little kiss from me as they went to bed at night. I knew the value of a nice hug for them—

and me—and decided that each morning when they came down, as well as before they went to school, upon returning from school, and each evening, they'd get a hug from Mom. Our little ones receive it so easily and naturally from us. Let us not forget the value of little moments for a hug for our older children, as well. It makes home a little happier for both of us.

## OBEDIENCE

Our second important cornerstone is obedience. "Obedience is the first law of heaven."

In our home we have a little saying:
> *I must do the things I ought*
> *Before I do the things I may;*
> *I am not fit for any task*
> *'Til I learn to obey.*

The real rewards in life are closed to us until we live this principle. It is interesting also, that a prerequisite for learning obedience to the principles of the Gospel and to our Heavenly Father, is that we learn obedience to parents in the home. The eternal success of our children is intricately connected to this important principle.

So we know how important it is, but how do we teach it? Very early!!! Children are most easily taught before the age of five. It becomes increasingly difficult after this age, though not impossible. It is important that the rules of the home be understood by the child, and then it is equally as important that as parents we make sure that those rules are consistently followed. Both are essential.

My own little boy one day kept going beyond the bounds of the carport after repeated instructions by me in an increasingly loud tone of voice, not to go past the carport. Finally, in exasperation, I hauled him in. With tears filling his eyes he asked, "What is da carpote?" Did I feel dumb!

Parents must have a clear picture of what is considered a law or rule in their home. If there is any fuzziness at all in the parents' minds, it will be even more unclear in the child's mind. Sit down together and formulate your rules. Dads and moms sometimes scream and carry on as children seem to wantonly breach rules. The fault often lies in the fact that the children aren't sure if this is just a momentary loss of sanity on the part of the parent, or if this rule is for real.

In our home we have written on construction paper in the shape of stone tablets, and placed on the refrigerator our "Ten Commandments of the House of Jacob." Here is clearly stated those rules and consequences that were the source of the most frequent "run-ins" in our family. These, of course, are superseded by those Ten Commandments given by the Lord that direct us in our path back to heaven, but these help to make a "heaven here on earth" in our home.

I was happy to find, after posting these, that my nagging had decreased by about half. I no longer found myself searching for some disastrous consequence when a child dumped his boots and coat just inside the door, or did not show up after school at the allotted time. They each knew, as well as I did, what the consequences were. They had helped to formulate the rules as well as the results of breaking them.

So we walked together, if need be, to the chart, read it, and they followed. There is still a need for parents to enforce, but the consistency is there, and consequently, the order.

A list of our commandments and the current consequences follows. (We had to adjust some of them as we found they weren't working as well as we had hoped.) Each family's will be different, just as each family's circumstances are different.

You will notice that we do not allow sassing or naughty words. Children must never be allowed to talk back or show disrespect to parents. That must always have some immediate follow-through, and our method of a tiny amount of hot pepper has cured it for the most part.

The important thing is for each family to decide on its own rules and consequences.

## THE TEN COMMANDMENTS OF THE HOUSE OF JACOB

1. Thou shalt be cheerful
1. Be witty if you can; Be pretty if you are; But be cheerful if it kills you.

2. Thou shalt come when called and obey cheerfully.
2. 10 points off (See chapter on Work)

3. Thou shalt be on time for prayer and devotional.
3. 10 points off.

4. Thou shalt not hit, fight, or quarrel.
4. Being put in the bathroom for five minutes together.

5. Thou shalt not eat outside the kitchen.
5. Vacuuming an area of the house assigned by Mom.

6. Thou shalt be home by 4:00.
6. Folding one batch of laundry.

7. Thou shalt keep all thy belongings put away.
7. Practicing putting them away ten times.

8. Thou shalt not say unkind or sassy words.
8. Dash of hot pepper on the tongue.

9. Thou shalt do all chores and practicing during the week.
9. No special treat at the end of the week without it.

10. Thou shalt have your room clean before school.
10. 25 points off

# Chapter VI

## Teaching Our Children to Work

Our third cornerstone for success is WORK, with its accompanying virtues of self-discipline, responsibility, perseverance, and appreciation, etc. Jim and I both came from homes where our parents worked very hard. Because of my childhood home being on a farm and Jim's father's occupation as a sheep rancher, we both were afforded the joys of hard work.

Unfortunately, most lifestyles today do not lend themselves to such luxury in the teaching of the important value of work. However, gaining this ability is equally as important today as in yesteryears. And the necessity of making the investment in time and effort on the part of parents in helping children learn to work cannot be overemphasized. But how?

Help Them to Feel Indispensable.

Initially, I believe each child should know that their contribution is essential to the success of his home. The deluge of written material and video presentations over television regarding the expense of child raising incurred by parents has had its negative effects on our children's attitudes. Children are now looked upon by most of society as liabilities, not assets.

For example, one magazine article states:

In the past, children were valued because of the work they could contribute to the family; sons were expected to work with their fathers in the field or in the business in town; and daughters were trained to do housework and to watch the younger children.

But today children are no longer economic advantages. Urban families are not made wealthy by an abundance of children; to the contrary, each new mouth to feed puts the family that much closer to the poverty line.

A skillful parent can, by virtue of his inspired and consistent teaching, eliminate that attitude, at least in the minds of his own family members.

Stories have been recorded of the marvelous response of young people to overwhelming challenges such as in saving a town from flooding; the youth could feel how vitally important their help was. In the past, the farming and cows having to be milked in order to provide sustenance for the family (as well as relief for the cow) was certainly a great incentive for the child because he knew, instinctively, by his parents' dependence upon him, that he was quite indispensable. I feel that it is this attitude that children need to receive in our homes today.

True, it is more difficult when the child knows the garbage won't flood the house if he forgets to take it out, and no one will starve to death if the petunias aren't weeded. But the parents still need to help each child feel that sense of indispensability in the home. This is important in helping a child gain a proper perspective and attitude toward his responsibilities.

## It Takes Time

Children do not learn to work by simply watching Mama and Daddy working. They learn to work by working with them. And teaching a child the work ethic takes time.

In the past, children observed and apprenticed with the parents in the accomplishing of the farm duties. Parents did not have to look for and make extra opportunities to teach this essential character trait; it came through the process of living. Many parents of today, however, look around at the time-saving conveniences in their homes—dishwasher, microwave, washer, vacuum—and suppose, perhaps, that their children can also be raised in some "quickie" way. But, alas, we find this is far from fact.

This attitude was recently brought out at a discussion held at BYU with the first occupant of the Camilla Eyring Kimball Chair of Home and Family Life visiting there. One audience member indicated that the quality of the time parents spend with their children is more important than the amount of time. Dr. Paolucci agreed but added, "There still has to be a minimum amount of time spent with the children. You can't have quality time without some quantity. And a lot of the learning takes place in the everyday things, the mundane things, the 'quantity time' things."

I would agree and strongly state that much of what we teach a child that lasts must be taught with quantity time. And how to work is one of those quantity-time activities.

Sometimes my children say to me, "But Mama, I don't feel like working! I'm always the one who works, and I'm tired of working!"

And I say, "Yes, and I sometimes don't feel like changing diapers, either. But in a few days, all of you would have to evacuate if Mama didn't."

So it's important that they learn that whether they feel like it or not, some things have to be done. So to work...

### Begin Early

In our home, we use a variety of methods for teaching children to work, and they change with time and circumstance, with the age of the child. Little children love visual evidence of what they have accomplished: a star, a sticker, or some small reward.

Children can start doing little daily duties at a very young age: four or five, or sometimes even three, if the child is fairly mature. But before this time, a child is already responsible for picking up his own toys and belongings and keeping his own room tidy. He has already gained the personal habits of having prayers, brushing teeth, etc.

As soon as a child learns to understand the words, "pick up your toys," he can begin to take this responsibility, often with the parents picking up with and assisting him. The important principle is to begin early, be consistent, and follow through. In other words, become involved yourself in the teaching of this character expanding virtue of work.

## The Point System

Jim and I have found that a point system works nicely with our children. We have seen this suggested many places and used successfully in several families we admire. This works on the premise of assigning a certain number of points for each task accomplished. (Children also must do many duties for which no points are given; this is also important.)

We tally each child's points in a book; it is like having a bank account to which they make deposits and from which they may take withdrawals when the need arises. This way, we have some control over the spending and there is a minimum of loss and waste.

Our four oldest children share a real checking account (House of Jacob Enterprises) on which they can write checks for their music lessons and other things (providing they have earned it, of course.)

Points are converted to pennies. A batch of dishes may be 15 points, cleaning an assigned area of the house 10 points, completing homework each night 10 points, and so on. The assignments can be made with the individual child's needs as the target areas. In some homes, a child struggling with reading might be awarded 10 points for reading so many minutes a day. (In our home, I have been tempted to take points off for this practice, as our children often stay up and read after I have tucked them in and I am anticipating a few moments of reading, myself.)

We require the children to fill out their own charts. If they do not keep up, I simply mark through two-day-old unfilled blanks and they forfeit the points. A sample of our job chart follows.

There are several ideas that Jim and I have found helpful for us. We sit down together before school starts and discuss assignments with the children. We then assign an area of the house a child will be in charge of for the entire school year. That way, in the evening when we say, "Room check in 15 minutes," and the children scatter to tidy up their area of the house, there is no question in their minds or ours where they should go.

We also assign two children to work on laundry for the school year, one to prepare lunches, another to help with breakfast. Our seven and six-year-olds, Jenet and Ellen, have had the assignment of setting the table and clearing out the dishwasher each morning and each afternoon after school. Richard has cleaned out the lunch boxes each day after school.

Some may think keeping the same assignments for so long is grossly unfair, without variety. I have learned, however, that just as parents must do routine tasks daily without ceasing, it is worthwhile for children to learn that important discipline in their lives. Our children have not objected as much with this system as when we were changing every week. It is far less confusing for me and seems for them, also.

(Sample Job Chart)

BECOMING BETTER

Name _____

Date _____

Family Goal: _____

My Goals for the Week: _____

Family Responsibility. We all: (No points)
    Say prayers
    Make bed
    Brush teeth (morning and night)
    Pick up own belongings

| INDIVIDUAL JOBS: | Sun | Mon | Tues | Wed | Thur | Fri | Sat |
|---|---|---|---|---|---|---|---|
| _____ ( ) | | | | | | | |
| _____ ( ) | | | | | | | |
| _____ ( ) | | | | | | | |
| _____ ( ) | | | | | | | |
| Memorization ( ) | | | | | | | |
| Bonus for doing all jobs and practicing ( ) | | | | | | | |
| MINUS POINTS: Quarreling ( ) | | | | | | | |
| Deafness to Mom or Dad ( ) | | | | | | | |
| Belongings out ( ) | | | | | | | |
| Other: ( ) | | | | | | | |

EXTRA POINTS:

COMMENTS:

## Simplify

Whenever possible, work can be simplified to create a minimum of confusion for family members.

For example, from a loosely woven mesh knit (used for making athletic duffle bags), I sewed large, rectangular bags—one for each child. A small plastic ring is attached to one corner for hanging on a nail or hook in the child's closet. When a child removes a pair of stockings, he puts it inside his own bag. (His name is on it.)

Once a week, the bags are washed with the stockings inside (Make sure the bag is large enough to allow free movement.), and are returned from the dryer to the bedrooms where the children mate them and return them to their drawers. No more lost socks. No more sock-mating marathons—and nobody even misses them at all!

Another way we cut down the confusion in a large family: Each of the older children is assigned a younger child to be a "guardian" over. This assignment is given even before the new baby is born. This has been a blessed relief on Sundays when the older child is responsible for seeing that his little "assignee" is ready for church. When we go places, the older child watches over and keeps the younger child safe and in toe. We have not found any problems with this system, though I worried some about the other children not feeling enough love or responsibility toward a child they were not the "guardian" over. This has not been evidenced at all, however, in the children's actions toward each other.

Jenet, our eight-year-old, just barely, will be the "guardian" over the new little tenth child we are expecting. She is so excited and thrilled at the prospect and reminds me frequently.

We learned, as I finished my year as National Young Mother, that we were expecting this tenth child. I wanted to share the good news with the children in some special way. So I baked a cake with a tin foil-wrapped message inside.

After dinner, Jim cut the cake, and when the note was found, he read it aloud to the children:

*To My Brothers and Sisters,*

*I want you to know the most wonderful news! I am coming to join our family! I have been feeling so excited, thinking about being with you again, 'cause I've missed you so much here in heaven.*

*I will be coming right near Christmas, so get ready with all of your love.*

*Thank you for wanting me.*

*Signed,*

*Your New Family Member Above*

Tears streamed down Jim's face as he read, though he already knew about the surprise (both the baby and the cake, of course). The children danced and shouted with joy and anticipation at this wonderful event. It never grows old; there are simply more to love and be loved...

# Chapter VII

## Teaching the Gospel of Jesus Christ

The fourth major responsibility we have as parents is to teach our children the Gospel of Jesus Christ. This is "a sure foundation, a foundation whereon if men build they cannot fall." (Hel. 10:12)

First of all, parents must themselves have a burning knowledge that this is true. We are promised "that when the devil shall send forth his mighty winds, yea, his shafts in the whirlwind, yea, when all his hail and his mighty storm shall beat upon you, it shall have no power over you to drag you down..." What a marvelous promise to live for! If we believe and have faith that the Lord is bound by His word, then we should do all in our power to make this promise a reality for our own children.

We need not raise our children with a fear that they will rebel and reject our teachings. The Lord's desire is that not one of our children be lost. He has, in this day, given numerous helps and a sure guide wherein we can bring our children back to Him. We, as parents, can literally build a spiritual protection or hedge around our homes. It takes a considerable amount of effort and prayer and time.

True, there are children who, through their agency, choose that path which leads to "endless misery and woe," for themselves and all who love them. I believe, though, that the Lord, almost without exception, sends us these children to succeed with, not to fail. If we are willing to do as the prophets have asked, each day, unrelenting, I know the rewards of a

"Forever Family" can be ours. Is the price we must pay in time and effort to have that eternal blessing worth it? Surely each parent who loves the Lord would join in crying out in a unanimous yes!

As parents in this Saturday evening of time, we have been blessed with help equal to the challenge we face in raising children in this crucial prelude to the Second Coming.

Our former and modern-day scriptures are specific in their instructions. Jim and I see four recurring themes. We are instructed to:

1—Have our family prayer, morning and evening, without fail.

2—Hold Family Home Evening each week with our children.

3—Study the scriptures daily with our children.

4—Encircle our homes with love.

In the last General Conference, April, 1983, President Gordon B. Hinckley admonished us to read one chapter per day from the Four Gospels and III Nephi until we completed it. Did we do it?

Many times as parents we become far more concerned with filling a child's physical, social, and emotional needs than his spiritual needs. What is eternal? What should our highest priority be for our children? If we are promised great blessings in our homes from reading the scriptures, then why do some of us deny our families for lack of commitment? If we want to insure our children's spiritual growth, we must do as we have been asked!

## Family Devotional

In speaking, I often have parents come up and look a little bewildered as they ask, "Where do we begin?" I always tell them that that which will bring the most immediate rewards and is fairly easy to instigate now is the family devotional. It is one of the greatest experiences we have each day as a family to help us fulfill the responsibility to teach our children the Gospel. We did this in my own family as we were growing up.

Oh, that every home could gather their families around them for such a time of sharing and learning. If every home in America would do this, there would be such an increase of love and loyalty and support!

We proceed in this way:

We first of all, sing a hymn together. One of the children often plays to accompany us, and another will lead. I think it important that children learn to confidently lead the hymns. Even our little ones enjoy beating the proper basic time patterns.

We sing the same hymn for some length of time until we have memorized all the words. This may not suit your family, but we enjoy having the children learn the words and message of the hymn until it belongs to them.

It would be appropriate to have family prayer at this time if you do not have it at your meals.

Next, we say a poem together. I have been a great lover of poetry for many years, and I love memorizing and collecting it. Our family devotional has been the ideal place and time to pass my love of poetry on to our children.

Our poems are sometimes very short. On the other hand, we've memorized some real classics that have taken us several weeks to learn. I cannot express in words how great the benefits have been from this little daily two to five-minute procedure.

The children have developed a great ability to memorize quickly. They have expressed to me numerous times, "Wow, Mom, I surely am glad that I can memorize quickly. I feel sorry for some of the kids in school who have such a hard time."

On numerous occasions, they have been able to speak on the spur of the moment and have given beautiful messages because of the great treasures of knowledge they have stored in their little minds. They have confidence and poise and they believe in their own ability.

Some of our favorite poems are included at the end of this book to get you started. Please try it! What a joy we can experience as we teach!

Next in our devotional is our scripture review. We have been through the Articles of Faith, Ten Commandments, Sermon on the Mount, and numerous other scriptures. These, too, are recited together as a family until they are learned. We have found our little five and six-year-olds memorize as quickly as our older children, so you need not fear that you have too large an age span.

We type all our poems and scriptures to be learned on 4x6 cards and place the current ones on the refrigerator with a magnetic holder. In the morning when we're ready to go over them, one of the children quickly retrieves them from the "fridge" and we're all set. I keep those that have been memorized in a file box. We now have two boxes that are quite full of those the children have learned and passed off.

We award points for memorization of the hymn, poem, and scripture—a little added incentive to get them completed.

Our last part of the devotional is the study of the scriptures. Jim is a tremendous teacher and knows and loves the scriptures himself. One year, as Jim was in school, I held it without his being there. It was not nearly as much fun or as easy, but we made it and grew from it.

I, too, was brought up in a home where daily scripture study was practiced and was blessed with parents who taught me a love for these precious books.

Jim keeps our scripture classes fun and exciting. He pretends he is an investigator and has the children teach him a certain principle, such as the Godhead or Baptism. He teaches them the scriptures that can be used and they, with ease, flip from one to another.

He assigns a child during the class, a little two or three minute mini sermon about a particular subject we are studying. With our new editions of the scriptures, even with limited knowledge of the scriptures, parents can teach their children through topics.

In the past, we have also read a certain amount of time, or a certain number of chapters. Whatever you feel comfortable with, begin; you can vary your approach as you go.

Our children love this time. As a family, we can feel (most of the time) the spirit of the Lord there with us. I have often thought, "If the Savior were to come to our home, I wish it could be now. He would be pleased with our efforts."

Some families may feel that there is no time for a family devotional. While growing up and taking early morning seminary, we had our family scripture time at 5:30 each morning. I knew that my parents had to have a great desire to teach us, or they would never have made that commitment, that sacrifice. It can be done!

My conviction is so strong regarding these devotionals, I wish I might somehow let each of you feel and know how deeply your own family and home can be blessed with the little joyous teaching time together. May you have the desire and the commitment to begin now to reap the rewards of your own family devotional.

# Chapter VIII

## Morningtime, Mealtime, Summertime

### Morningtime

Learn the value of the morning hours! It takes real discipline, "mind over mattress," and determination on the part of the parents. But the results of order and accomplishment are worth it many times over.

To have a successful morning, it is important that the home has been tidied and prepared the night before. We have the children tidy their assigned areas before they go to bed, so the house is ready to put to bed, as well.

Jim and I believe there should be time each morning for the children to get themselves ready, their rooms tidy, a chore completed, some time to practice on their particular talent, a nourishing breakfast, and receive spiritual nourishment through our family devotional.

Planning together as a family should help each child understand his duties in the morning. This alleviates much confusion and contention.

In our home, because of having animals to care for and practicing to be done by six of our children, we arise very early. We have had to move this time up as the years progressed and our family size has increased.

We awaken the older children at 5:00 a.m. Our oldest three girls dress and come down to practice their instruments. (We have two on the violin and one on cello.) Jim and Richy go out to care for the animals, milk the cow, gather eggs, etc. I prepare breakfast and one of the children assists in preparation of the lunches.

The next two children get up at 6:00 a.m. and come down—after dressing and making beds—to set the table, clear out the dishwasher and proceed to practice their violin and harp. Richy comes in and, after dressing for school, begins practicing his guitar. It works quite well and requires only a minimum of nagging—usually.

Breakfast is at 7:15. We hold our family devotional immediately after breakfast and just before the children leave for school.

When the children leave for school, they leave the house ready for the day, and their own bodies and spirits and minds refreshed, challenged and strengthened. It is a great feeling for all of us!

## Mealtime

Mealtimes may be horrendously horrible or absolutely delightful. We have had our share of both. I read Boyd K. Packer's book, Teach Ye Diligently, and liked his idea of feeding the children their supper right after they arrive home from school. I could see that was something that could be especially helpful in our home, as Jim had no regular hours. This leaves me with the responsibility of making mealtime in the evening bearable, and even enjoyable, without Daddy's assistance.

We have used a variety of methods. We have had each child report on something he learned that day, as well as one thing he did to make another person happy. This has continued to work well and takes only a small amount of time, even with many reporting.

We have used mealtime as a time to read to the children. When our daddy is home, we like the table free for conversation, but the children don't seem to mind us reading when he is gone. I have also used tapes of scriptures stories or other interesting stories. We have listened to music on the stereo while we eat.

Last year I gave out spelling words during the mealtime from their big spelling bee list from school. Even our younger ones enjoyed our little mini spelling bees at the table and joined right in. Jenet came home two days ago with an award for the best speller in the second grade class. Those mealtimes proved to be an advantage to her.

Richard and Linda Eyre have an entire program, "Teaching Children Responsibility," that outlines questions and answers about a great many topics designed for mealtime use. What a boon this can be to our families as we learn history, geography, science, literature, etc., together.

We have a map displayed near our table and use it to point out where our loved ones are, or the location of events that are happening in the world. Home should be a place designed with learning in mind. That atmosphere in such a home is stimulating and inspiring for parents and children alike.

Evaluate your mealtimes and plan now to make them memorable, not for the number of glasses of milk spilled, or peas smashed, but for the great learning and fun that can be had with those who love the best.

## Summertime

Summer days, after school has adjourned, brings great change in our family's routine. We change room cleaning assignments, practicing hours, recreation time (both of which increase). A greater emphasis is placed on the development of certain house and yard skills that cannot have adequate time spent on them during the school term. We get to sleep in later and stay up longer than during the school year.

Before the first summer day arrives, we have another family meeting where we work out our new schedules. We assign meal preparation days, and doing dishes days, and even which piano will be practiced on at what time for each child.

A little school time for the younger preschool children continues through the summer. I usually assign this to one of our middle children, who thoroughly delights in being a teacher for the summer. If there are specific areas a child needs to review or work on during the summer, a specific number of pages or an allotted time is assigned daily for this purpose. The children are not allowed free time until after completion of all practicing and chores—and then they may not leave until after our quiet time at 2:00 p.m.

The children absolutely thrive under a schedule that they themselves help to make. They love to feel they have accomplished as well as we like them to. They appreciate their leisure time to a much greater degree and relish the time they can play and chum with friends.

I love the summer to work on teaching homemaking skills to both our daughters and sons. They like to plan the menus, fix the meals, and learn to clean up properly afterward. It takes a great amount of time and effort, but when you can sit down to a lovely meal prepared completely, tastefully, and happily by your nine, ten, and eleven or twelve-year-old, what a feeling of joy it is!

We also have assigned time daily for yard and garden work. Each child has his own specific area for which he is responsible. Jim works with them teaching them the "how to" of keeping a yard and garden lovely. Then at harvest time, we work together in freezing, canning, and eating of this work of all our hands.

*Homemade Joy from the House of Jacob*

At the conclusion of the summer, it is fun to have an Awards Ceremony to celebrate and congratulate each child for his accomplishments. One lovely mother has done this for many years with her children and says it is as fun as Christmas. They display the articles the children have sewn, painted, canned, written, played, etc. She awards prizes such as socks for school, new music books, clothes, etc. What a fun way to finish up a successful, growing summer.

# Chapter IX

## A Love for Learning

I had one sweet grandma who, even in her nineties, would read many, many books. She loved learning, and she taught me to love learning and have an insatiable appetite for continuing to read and to learn and to gain wisdom.

In contrast, one woman, a bank teller, said: "One Saturday, as my husband and I were driving to town, we crossed under a bridge on which was a speeding train. I said, 'Look at the choo-choo.' My husband looked at me and smiled—I had begun to think like a child. I knew that I had to go back to work. My children were shrinking my brain."

What a distorted perspective! Rather than spending her time, thoughts, and energies in expanding and enriching her children's minds, she felt that the children were shrinking her own mind. Thus, she felt a need to leave them and go to work.

There is so much we can teach our children in the short time they are with us!

One thing I learned as a child was an appreciation for the value of time. Both Mother and Daddy emphasized this and helped us find numerous ways to spend our time wisely. The following are some ideas that we have used to help the children develop themselves and to make our home happier by being able to accomplish more. "By small and simple things are great things brought to pass." (Alma 37:6) Sometimes the little things we do over and over bring the greatest rewards.

Use the spare moments well. Hair combing time (with seven daughters, this takes a chunk out of each morning) can be spent in memorizing scriptures, poems, having the child read to me, or with the little ones taking barrettes out and learning the colors.

Use the refrigerator for putting up letters, colors, numbers, etc., to help the pre-schooler learn. My little boy is constantly on the run and so, as he runs by, we have him name the letters or numbers on display that week.

While doing dishes, we often learn songs. The girls think (and I know) that any task is made easier with a "spoonful of sugar." We are a singing family, and the children know a great number of songs simply from using the moments that our hands are busy but our minds are free. Also, as we travel we learn many poems and songs as we go. If the children are singing, they're not fighting.

I use my lullaby time at night to sing songs I want the children to learn. This past summer, as I was Primary chorister, I learned the songs along with the children. We did it as I sang to them at night, letting them listen and listen.

I record poems or stories or songs on the cassette recorder. As they play or eat, I simply push the button. This saves time for me as I don't have to sit down specifically for the purpose of teaching a poem. They hear it and are soon saying it themselves.

The children started in Suzuki several years ago, and I suppose I learned the value of repetition from this program. We would play the record over and over while the children were eating or playing with their toys. The children who needed to hear the record progressed very rapidly in their violin playing. But what amazed us was hearing our one-year-old singing the melodies over and over—long before each could talk. The children all sing well, and we attribute part of that to the great exposure to music that they receive, much of it incidentally.

Never underestimate the mind of a child. This little fact has been borne out more strongly as we have each new little one. They comprehend and are learning so much more than we realize. The little two, three, and four-year-olds can be memorizing, developing their minds and talents—if the mother will simply be prepared and willing to help them. It is really a challenge, but the more we become excited about being a truly "professional" mother and using our time to teach our children, the more we ourselves feel fulfilled. It makes being a mother the most challenging and rewarding of all careers.

Last year our little five-year-old, Ellen, came to me and said, "Mama, I have to give a poem in kindergarten this week, and I can't decide whether to give 'If' by Kipling, or 'The Psalm of Life' by Longfellow, or 'My Kingdom,' by Louisa May Alcott. But I think I will give 'The Road Not Taken,' by Robert Frost."

She went to school and stood before her little kindergarten class and said, "I will now say 'The Road Not Taken' by Robert Frost."

And her teacher said, "And I will now climb Mount Everest in a single bound!" But Ellen recited the poem...

A wealth? Oh, yes! You see, the diapers and the dishes and the floors all have to be redone over and over again. But the teaching lasts forever!

And we must remind ourselves: If our mind was the only book our children could read, what would it contain? How important it is that our young women of today—our young mothers—are educated and knowledgeable! Why? Because when you educate a woman, you educate a family. Oh, to have educated mothers in our home—mothers who are willing to teach and train their children.

Where are our great scientists and musicians and artists, historians and leaders of tomorrow going to come from?

They're going to come from homes where mothers, educated and knowledgeable and talented and gifted in those areas teach their children—that's where they're going to come from. The most capable women in the world need to be in their homes teaching their children to be strong, great leaders for our America tomorrow.

### Bedtime-Reading Time

"Richer than I you will never be, for I had a mother who read to me."

Almost every evening I sit in the hallway, after the children are in their own beds, and read them a story. What a sweet feeling to have all your flock gathered around and safe and snug, enjoying the warmth and love of a story from Dad or Mom.

We have been through all the Little House on the Prairie series, All of a Kind Family, Five Little Peppers, A Story to Tell, Book of Mormon Stories for Children, Scripture Stories, Spencer W. Kimball, the Outstanding Stories series by Leon Hartshorn, Louisa May Alcott books, and numerous other classics checked out from the Library or purchased.

Our oldest is 13, and she still moans when the reading time is over. Surely it is one of the sweetest times of the day in our home.

# Chapter X

## The Rich Heritage of Music

In my childhood home, next to having the blessings of the Gospel, I think I have appreciated most the joy we received through music—what a rich heritage! Mother often used to say she had us sing to keep us from fighting, for we couldn't do them both at the same time. We disproved her theory a few times, but basically, it proved to be true.

I was the oldest girl and took great delight for many years in preparing special programs for Mom and Dad on their special days. We would learn poems, sing songs, do pantomimes, make up stories, relate incidents from their lives, write special tributes.

We used our fireplace ledge for our performing stage so much as children, that as soon as we would step on it, our feet would dance and our smiles light up, and the show would begin.

As children growing up, we would prepare a program each year for our school teachers. We would send them little homemade invitations and they would come to our home and watch our family program, which included little solos by each child. Many of my former teachers have said that was one of the highlights of their teaching years.

Mom and Dad did many special things that helped us experience the joy of sharing our talents with others.

We three oldest girls began singing together when I was about fourteen and they about thirteen and twelve. At first we sang at family gatherings and then at small local programs.

More opportunities began to come to us, and before too long we were singing almost every Sunday in different sacrament meetings in the area.

Later, we were joined by my younger three sisters, making a sextet. Mother inquired of Kurt Weinsinger at BYU if he would consider teaching us, all together. He replied that he probably would not, as he didn't coach groups like that, but he was willing to listen to us.... He coached us for the next two years without even any monetary compensation, saying it was such an honor for him to be able to work with such "lovely girls." He was very gracious and good to us.

Meanwhile, our opportunities for performing continued to increase. We presented shows in various locations throughout the western states. In reading my mother's journal recently, I was amazed at the multitudes of performances—there must have been hundreds of them!

Generally, it was Mother (and our accompanist) who took us to the programs. We had such great times together! Mother often had difficulty in finding addresses, and we were always getting lost, it seemed. Those experiences, practicing and performing with my sisters, became a great cohesive force in our lives and contributed a great deal to the closeness we feel even now.

One of the most memorable times was when we gave a private concert for President David O. McKay at his home in Huntsville, Utah. We sang "Oh That I Were an Angel," and President McKay leaned over to Sister McKay and said, "Mama, that sounds just like the angels singing." He kissed each of us. What a choice memory, shared by six young girls!

When we went on BYU Education Week tours, our brothers joined the group. Daddy also joined us on those family tours. By this time we had become "semi-professional" and were known as The Andersen Sisters. We appeared on television several times. During our college years, we also toured with the BYU Program Bureau.

When I was engaged to Jim, during the Christmas holidays we did 18 to 20 Christmas programs—that was our courtship.

The Andersen Sisters went to Hollywood and performed on a nationally televised college talent show. We were approached by two agents, each impressed enough to offer his services in promoting our career.

By this time, however, I was newly married and another sister was engaged to be married. The group disbanded...but those many, marvelous experiences together have provided memories that will last us a lifetime!

\* \* \* \* \* \*

How grateful I am to have been born in a home where good music was listened to, played, and sung, both individually and as a family. This refinement carried over into our selection of books, movies and other entertainment.

Music effects the spirituality of the soul and the sensitivity to the Spirit of the Lord. It is an important way in which parents can teach their children to love the good and the beautiful in life and to seek after that which is "lovely, of good report, and praiseworthy."

Music has many obvious benefits as well as some that perhaps only those who experience the joy of creating and expressing feelings through their music can know. Music is a science, music is mathematical, music is a foreign language, music is history, music is physical education. In addition, music provides opportunities to develop self-discipline, poise, confidence, and creativity. Good music helps develop our sensitivity, our love of beauty, our appreciation for nature. It helps us develop greater love and compassion, gentleness, and goodness. Good music gives to us, in short, a more "abundant life."

My definition of good music would have to be that which is uplifting, inspiring, and in harmony with the soul.

Parents must initially realize the power that music can exert on themselves and on their children. Dr. Reid Nibley stated:

"The spoken word must pass through areas of the brain controlling rational thought where it is screened for content and then evaluated. But music simply passes by the rational mind and directly affects the senses. For example, individuals may find themselves with a foot tapping automatically as a band marches by, or with a lump in the throat or tears in the eyes when hearing certain numbers."

Music exerts an influence on our digestive, secretory, circulatory, nutritive, and respiratory functions. A dear friend of mine who was a young girl growing up in Germany during Hitler's reign speaks of the power music played in moving the masses to accept and even enthusiastically cheer for this man and his purposes.

The acid rock music of today exerts great influence over the minds of young people as evidenced by the huge, brutally immoral, and horrifying spectacles found at the mass rock concerts. It has been openly and repeatedly emphasized by numerous rock artists that they compose and perform in order to add fire to the wave of homosexuality, drugs, sex perversions, alienation to parents and authority, atheism, and satan worship. We are not dealing with some passing fancy with our teens; this is real. It is designed specifically to destroy the virtue and high moral values of the young.

If in our homes we are presently disturbed by the quality of music being listened to, I might suggest having your family read Pop Music and Morality by Lex de Azevedo.

What can we do? Initially, we train our children to love the good. Just as a love for the scriptures is developed over time and is accompanied by a refinement of the soul, so with good music. For years in discussing this with parents, they have repeatedly told me, "Just wait until your children are teenagers; you'll see."

Well, now I can see. They are extremely selective in their music. True, they hear the other when they are with friends. But when they choose, it is always that which they have through the years been trained to love.

In numerous studies it has been found that children develop their taste for music during the pre-school years. Mothers have looked at me with an incredible expression and replied, "But my son never once heard the Beatles or Ozzie Osborn as a child—and he has the worst addiction to rock music imaginable now."

What we sometimes fail to realize is that we may develop a "taste" for certain music—or we may fail to develop a taste for that which is refined and beautiful. And so, often, when the pressure is on from peers, the child will choose that which is popular, not proper.

When a child's main exposure each day has been "Sesame Street" or "General Electric Co.," you may be sure his taste in music will not be of the highest caliber as he grows up. As parents we must make a conscious effort to expose our children often and consistently to music that refines and lifts the soul.

Another thing we have done is to begin music lessons early with the children so that they, themselves play the great classics by composers such as Bach, who said that the aim and final reason of all music should be nothing but the glory of God and the refreshment of the spirit.

I would encourage all parents to provide the opportunity for their children to play a musical instrument. If finances are a problem, teachers will sometimes be willing and even eager to trade baked goods, sewing, or other services for the lessons. Your willingness to sacrifice for the enrichment of your child will be repaid many times over!

There are additional ways in which we can help provide opportunities for our children. They can prepare special little programs for holidays and other special days. This is a great way to get the children to prepare a number to present without the pressure of a "recital" performance. It is also a great time to share poems and scriptures learned in family devotional, as well as a time for those who love to dramatize to express their talents.

Frequently people ask me, "Where did your children learn such confidence and ease in their performing?" I jokingly (only half-jokingly) tell them that we hired the grandparents to come and listen and then friends and neighbors, offering free 7-Up at every performance. Grandparents are the greatest "guinea pigs", as they think your children are as wonderful as you do and delight in every little part they perform. Don't hesitate to invite other loved ones or friends to share a little evening of fun and refreshments. A good time is had by all and there is much learning and love that is shared.

Dr. Reid Nibley gives several suggestions to help us develop a higher musical taste:

1—Listen to classical music on the radio. (That would shock a few friends.)
2—Go to concerts and recitals.
3—Buy a classical record and play it often.
4—Listen to worshipful music on the sabbath.

It might be well to consider as a family what type of music the Savior would have playing in His home. There are some homes I fear He would pass by, simply because the music blaring from within would be uninviting to Him.

Finally, in a loving way, help the children to know how that type of music affects your own spirit and that of your home. They each have a responsibility to make it possible for the Spirit of the Lord to dwell in the home. The music designed to promote that which is evil would certainly drive that spirit of love away.

Teach the hymns to your family through the family devotional. Sing together the songs of Zion. Start now to develop refined tastes in your children and work with older ones to wean them away from that which is designed to destroy their spirituality and sensitivity. May you be blessed and encouraged in their efforts.

# Chapter XI

## Some of Our Favorite Poems

### The Road Not Taken
*Robert Frost*

Two roads diverged in a yellow wood,
And sorry I could not travel both
And be one traveler, long I stood
And looked down one as far as I could
To where it bent in the undergrowth;

Then took the other, as just as fair,
And having perhaps the better claim,
Because it was grassy and wanted wear
Though as for that, the passing there
Had worn them really about the same.

And both that morning equally lay
In leaves no step had trodden black
Oh, I kept the first for another day
Yet knowing how way leads on to way
I doubted if I should ever come back.

I shall be telling this with a sigh
Somewhere ages and ages hence;
Two roads diverged in a wood, and I
I took the one less traveled by,
And that has made all the difference.

"Pure hearts in pure homes are always in whispering distance of heaven." —*David O. McKay*

*Some of Our Favorite Poems*

## JUST FOR FUN

### My Hands

Sometimes my hands are naughty,
And so my mama says,
"I will have to spank them
and send them off to bed."
And so, little hands, be careful
Of everything you do.
Because if you have to go to bed,
I have to go there too!

### A Smile

A smile is catching
Like measles, they say
So you better watch out;
I have one today.

A smile is catching
And so I suppose
A big one could pop out,
Right under your nose.

### My Nose

It doesn't breathe
It doesn't smell
It doesn't feel so very well
I'm discouraged with my nose,
The only thing it does is blows!

*Homemade Joy from the House of Jacob*

### Tobacco

Tobacco is a dirty weed
And from the devil it doth proceed.
It picks your pockets
And burns your clothes
And makes a chimney out of your nose.

### The Owl
*Edward Richards*

There was an old owl who sat in an oak,
The more he sat, the less he spoke.
The less he spoke, the more he heard.
Why can't we be like that wise old bird?

### Mud

Mud is very nice to feel
All squishy, squashy between the toes
I'd rather step in squishy mud
Than smell a yellow rose.
Nobody else, but the rose bush knows
How nice mud feels between the toes.

## HOLIDAYS

### Mr. Turkey

"Good morning, Mr. Turkey, I've come
   to talk to you.
But you're so big and gobbly, you
   kind of scare me too.
I have something to tell you

## Some of Our Favorite Poems

That I think you ought to hear.
It's just like this, Mr. Turkey,
Thanksgiving's awfully near.

It surely comes tomorrow,
That's what my mama said.
And if you're here tomorrow,
Mr. Turkey, you'll be dead.
It makes me feel real sorry
What I heard my mama say
So I came right out to tell you:
Mr. Turkey, run away!!"

### Snow
*Dorothy Alids*

The fenceposts wear marshmallow hats
On a snowy day,
Bushes in their night gowns
Are kneeling down to pray
And all the trees have silver skirts
And want to dance away.

### Long, Long Ago

Wind through the olive trees
Softly did blow
Around little Bethlehem
Long, long ago.

Sheep on the hillside lay
Whiter than snow
Shepherds were watching them
Long, long ago.

Then from a happy sky

*Homemade Joy from the House of Jacob*

Angels bent low
Singing their songs of joy
Long, long ago.

For in a manger bed
Cradled we know
Christ came to Bethlehem
Long, long ago.

### Bundles

A bundle is a funny thing
It always sets me to wondering
For whether it is thin or wide
You never know just what's inside
Especially on Christmas week
Temptation is so great to peek
Now wouldn't it be much more fun
If shoppers carried their things undone?

### If I Had Been a Shepherd Boy

If I had been a shepherd boy
On that very special night
Tending sheep upon the hillside
I'd have seen the angels bright.

I'd have heard the angels singing
Of what happened in the town
I'd have left my flock with someone
So that I could hurry down.

I'd have seen the humble manger
Where the newborn baby lay
And the silent cattle watching
As they munched sweet smelling hay.

*Some of Our Favorite Poems*

## CHARACTER

### Beyond
*Kent Porter*

Incredible it is
That as we approach our boundaries
Our boundaries disappear
And there, in the midst
Where we thought capacity ceased
We find ourselves beginning.

We, capable beyond all thought
Of only coping
And here, only here
Pushed beyond ourselves
Can we find ourselves.

Oh that we could remember
Always our divinity
Reaching beyond our stretch of sinew
Into cool faith
Beyond.

### I Am an Eagle

I am an eagle; I live for the challenge
Created by visions that reach to the sky.
From high in the heavens I beckon,
"Come and join me."

There's so little difference between you and I.
For all those who see me and all who believe in me
Share in the freedom I feel when I fly.

### *Homemade Joy from the House of Jacob*

Come onward and upward and forward together.
Sail over the mountains and up to the stars,
And reach for the heavens and hope for the future.
Be all that we can be and more than we are.

### What Really Matters

My mother says she doesn't care
About the color of my hair
Of if my eyes are blue or brown
Or if my nose turns up or down.
She says she doesn't care for things like that.
    It really doesn't matter.

My mother says she doesn't care
If I'm dark or if I'm fair
Or if I'm thin or if I'm fat
She says she doesn't care for things like that.
    It really doesn't matter.

But if I cheat or tell a lie
Or do mean things to make folks cry,
Or if I'm rude or impolite
And do not try to do what's right,
    Then that really does matter.

It isn't looks that makes one great.
It's character that seals your fate.
It's what you are within your heart, you see,
That makes or mars your destiny.
    And that really does matter!

### My Kingdom
*Louisa May Alcott*

A little kingdom I possess,

Where thoughts and feeling dwell;
And very hard the task I find
Of governing it well.
For passion tempts and troubles me.
A wayward will misleads,
And selfishness its shadow casts
On all my words and deeds.

How can I learn to rule myself,
To be the child I should,
Honest, and brave, nor ever tire
Of trying to be good?
How can I keep a sunny soul
To shine along life's way?
How can I tune my little heart
To sweetly sing all day?

Dear Father, help me with the love
That casteth out my fear!
Teach me to lean on thee and feel
That thou art very near;
That no temptation is unseen
No childish grief too small.
Since Thou, with patience infinite
Doth sooth and comfort all.

I do not ask for any crown
But that which all may win:
Nor seek to conquer any world
Except the one within.
Be thou my guide until I find
Led by a tender hand
The happy kingdom in myself,
And dare to take command.

### Homemade Joy from the House of Jacob

>  It matters not if you try and fail
>     And try and fail again.
>  It matters much if you try and fail
>     And fail to try again.

### If
#### *Rudyard Kipling*

If you can keep your head when all about you
Are losing theirs and blaming it on you;
If you can trust when all men doubt you,
But make allowance for their doubting, too;
If you can wait and not be tired by waiting,
Or being lied about, don't deal in lies,
Or being hated, don't give way to hating,
And yet don't look too good, nor talk too wise.

If you can fill the unforgiving minute
With sixty seconds' worth of distance run,
Yours is the Earth and everything that's in it,
And—which is more—you'll be a Man, my son!

### Winning

>  It takes a little courage
>     And a little self-control
>  And some grim determination
>     If you want to reach a goal.
>  It takes a deal of striving
>     And a firm and stern-set chin,
>  No matter what the battle,
>     If you're really out to win.
>  There's no easy path to glory
>     There's no rosy road to fame,

## Some of Our Favorite Poems

Life, however we may view it,
    Is no simple parlor game;
But its prizes call for fighting,
    For endurance and for grit,
For a rugged disposition
    And a "don't-know-when-to-quit."

You must take a blow or give on,
    You must risk and you must lose,
And expect that in the struggle
    You will suffer from a bruise,
But you musn't wince or falter,
    If a fight you once begin,
Be a man and face the battle—
    That's the only way to win.

*Homemade Joy from the House of Jacob*

### The Grumble Family

There is a family nobody likes to meet,
They live, it is said, on Complaining Street
In the city of Never-Are-Satisfied
The River of Discontent beside.

They growl at that, and they growl at this;
Whatever comes, there is something amiss;
And whether their station be high or humble
They are known by the name of Grumble.

The weather is always too hot or too cold,
Summer and winter alike they scold;
Nothing goes right with the folks you meet
Down on the gloomy Complaining Street.

They growl at the rain, and they growl at the sun;
In fact, their growling is never done.
And if everything pleased them, there isn't a doubt
They'd growl that they'd nothing to grumble about.

And the worst thing is that if anyone stays
Among them too long, he will learn their ways,
And before he dreams of the terrible umble
He's adopted into the family of Grumble.

So it is wisest to keep our feet
From wandering into Grumbling Street
And never to growl whatever we do
Lest we be mistaken for Grumblers, too.


## Stick to Your Task

Stick to your task 'til it sticks to you!
Beginners are many, but enders are few.
Honor, power, place and praise
Will always come to the one who stays.

Stick to your task, 'til it sticks to you!
Grin at it, sweat at it, smile at it too.
For out of the grin and the sweat and the smile
Will come life's victories after awhile.

## Homemade Joy from the House of Jacob

No matter if you're quicker
Or slower than the rest.
The main thing when you're working
Is to do your very best.

### Psalm of Life
*Longfellow*

Not enjoyment, and not sorrow,
Is our destined end or way;
But to act, that each tomorrow
Finds us farther than today
Let us, then, be up and doing,
With a heart for any fate;
Still achieving, still pursuing,
Learn to labor and to wait.

Boys flying kites haul in their white-winged birds.
You can't do that when you're flying words.
Careful with fire is good advice, you know.
Careful with words is ten times doubly so.
Thoughts unexpressed may sometimes fall back dead.
But God himself can't kill them once they're said.
*Will Carlton*

You may have riches and wealth untold—
Caskets of jewels and baskets of gold.
But richer than I, you will never be,
For I had a mother who read to me.
*Thomas Carlyle*

## Some of Our Favorite Poems

### A Mother's Prayer

Oh, give me patience when tiny hands
Tug at me with their small demands.
And give me gentle and smiling eyes;
Keep my lips from sharp replies.

And let not fatigue, confusion, or noise
Obscure my vision of life's fleeting joys,
So when, years later, my house is still—
No bitter memories its rooms may fill.

### I Love You, Mother

"I love you, Mother," said little John;
Then forgetting his work, his cap went on
And he was off to the garden swing,
Leaving her the water and wood to bring.

"I love you, Mother," said rose Nell.
"I love you more than tongue can tell."
Then she teased and pouted full half the day,
'Til her mother rejoiced when she went to play.

"I love you, Mother," said little Fan.
"Today I'll help you all I can.
How glad I am that school doesn't keep."
So she rocked the baby 'til it fell asleep.

Then stepping softly, she fetched the broom
And swept the floor and tidied the room.
Busy and happy all day was she,
Helpful and happy as a child could be.

"I love you, Mother," again they said,
Three little children going to bed.
How do you think the mother guessed
Which of them really loved her best?

*Homemade Joy from the House of Jacob*

### Mother Magic
*Jean Brabham McKinney*

There's magic about Mother
That goes with her everywhere
Like fragrance floating on the wind
And music in the air.

There's magic in the way she lights
A dark and lonely room;
In cakes and cookies that she bakes,
In sweeping with a broom.

Her magic helps her mend our toys
And kiss away our tears.
This magic is her love, I guess,
Enduring through the years.

### My Daddy's Gift

My daddy said the other day
He wanted just one gift.
It wasn't a hat, or a fancy tie
Or a book or a handkerchief.

"All that I shall want," said he,
"And Mother wants it too,
Is just to have you kind and sweet,
To keep you good and true."

And so, though I'm a little girl,
I'll try to do my part,
Each day to bring this precious gift,
To cheer my daddy's heart.

### My Daddy's Hands
*Jean Brabham McKinney*

My daddy's hands are large and long,
His slender fingers, straight and strong.

But they can mend the smallest toy
Broken by a little boy.

They work outdoors for me all day;
They sow, they reap, they toss fresh hay.
And in the sandpile, out of sand,
They build dream castles, tall and grand.

His hand on mine, heads high with pride,
My dad and I walk side by side.

## I Like to See
### *Mabel Watts*

I like to see flowers, and beetles and things.
I like to see baby birds try out their wings.
I like to see ships bouncing out on the sea—
I like to pretend that the captain is me!

I like to see puppies, and kittens and mice.
Sunbeams and showers, and seashells are nice.
I like to see bright-colored leaves as they fall,
But I like to see Daddy come home Best of all!

## Sharing Time
### *Della D. Provost*

My daddy and I have a sharing time almost every day.
Sometimes it's a story he reads to me.
Sometimes it's a game we play.
Sometimes it's a walk we like to take.
Sometimes it's a show we see.
Sometimes it's something he helps me to make,
Like a playhouse under a tree.
But it isn't so much what we choose to do
Or play, or make, or see,

## Homemade Joy from the House of Jacob

It's just that we have a sharing time.

### My Mother's Hands
*Mabel Jones Gabbott*

My mother's hands are kind and good,
They work all day for me;
They cook my food and wash my clothes,
And push the swing for me.

At night I love my mother's hands,
They tuck me into bed;
They pull the covers up just so,
And gently pat my head.

### My Grandmother
*Regina Sauro*

Her soft hands are gentle
And full of wrinkles.
Her sweet face is kind
And lined with crinkles.
Her laughing eyes
Always shine with twinkles.

### My Granny

My granny's hair is grayin'
She has pretty, shiny eyes.
My granny can knit mittens;
My granny can bake pies.

But today she told me something,
I never thought could be.
A granny said that once she was

## Some of Our Favorite Poems

A little girl like me.

### Walking With Grandpa
*Della D. Provost*

I take grandpa's hand
And we go for a walk;
We listen and look,
We stop and we talk.
We take lots of time
For laughs and for jokes
'Cause we don't have to hurry
Like most other folks.

## Post Script:

I learned today, after this book had already gone to the printer, that the fetus I am carrying is no longer living. This is an entirely new experience for me, rather a strange feeling.... We are sad and disappointed, yet are trying to be positive and hopeful for the future.

I will learn from this experience. I will, perhaps, feel ever more empathy for those who have a more difficult time than I have had in the past, in bringing children into the world.

I feel a renewed gratitude for the nine that we already have. And never will I take for granted the blessing of having a normal, uneventful pregnancy.

Heavenly Father has blessed us so abundantly and in so many ways, including giving us opportunities to have new experiences, to grow, and to learn....

It is much easier to dream than to make those dreams become reality. It is easier for me to remember: "Her voice was ever soft, gentle and low, an excellent thing in a woman," (Shakespeare)—when the children are all playing in Grandma's back yard than when they are in the midst of yet another childish squabble.

I have had times when I have retired for the night hoping that our children would somehow turn out with any good qualities at all and thinking that if they did, it would certainly be in spite of, and not because of, me.

I have wished at times, such as when one child has slugged another on stage, in front of a large audience, that I could hide under the piano or disappear somehow. They too, I have felt the overwhelming joy of seeing one of our children perform magnificently with poise and confidence, something on which

## Post Script:

we, together, had worked very hard. I have felt then that it was all worth it.

As with our Father in Heaven, our ultimate goal as parents is to "bring to pass the immortality and eternal life" of our children, as God gives us strength and inspiration to do so.

What we do truly does matter. And as we desire to improve, while continuing to do those things we already know will eventually bring eternal joy, then we will surely come to know of that peace which passeth all understanding, that joy which is full and eternal.

And when we make mistakes, may we still realize that our Father is there to help, for He wants us to succeed in this—the most important and challenging responsibility that can come to us in this life. May you find your own homemade joy!

With Love,
The House of Jacob

2nd Edition Footnote
Our 10th child, Shirley Lynette was born June 5, 1984!

Made in the USA
San Bernardino, CA
21 July 2020